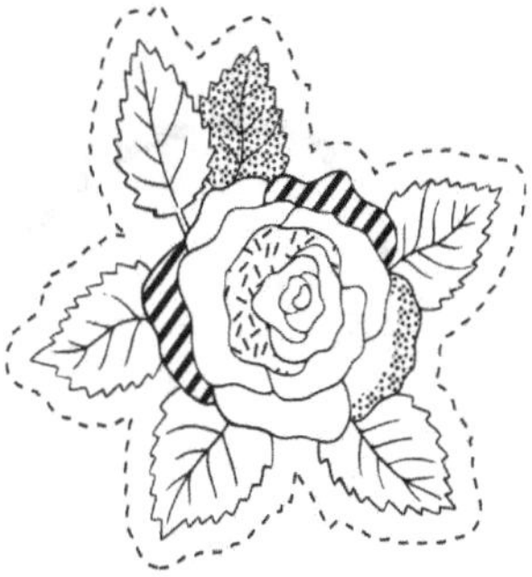

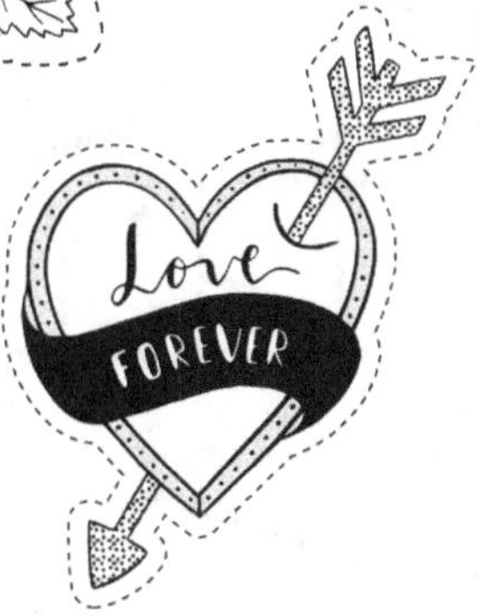

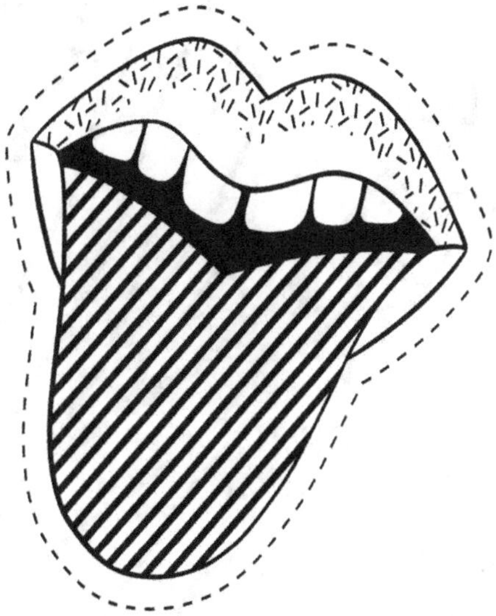

Name

Date

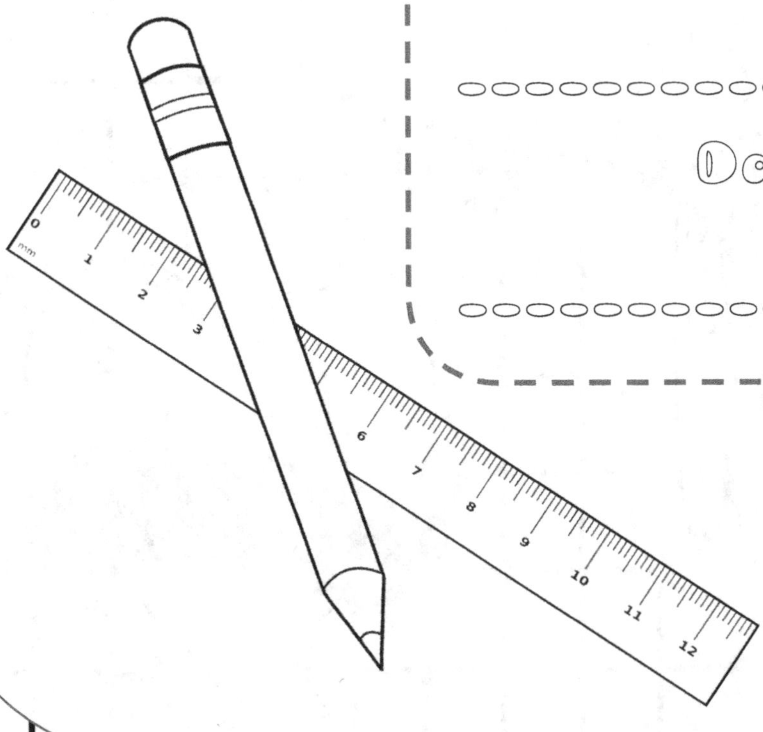

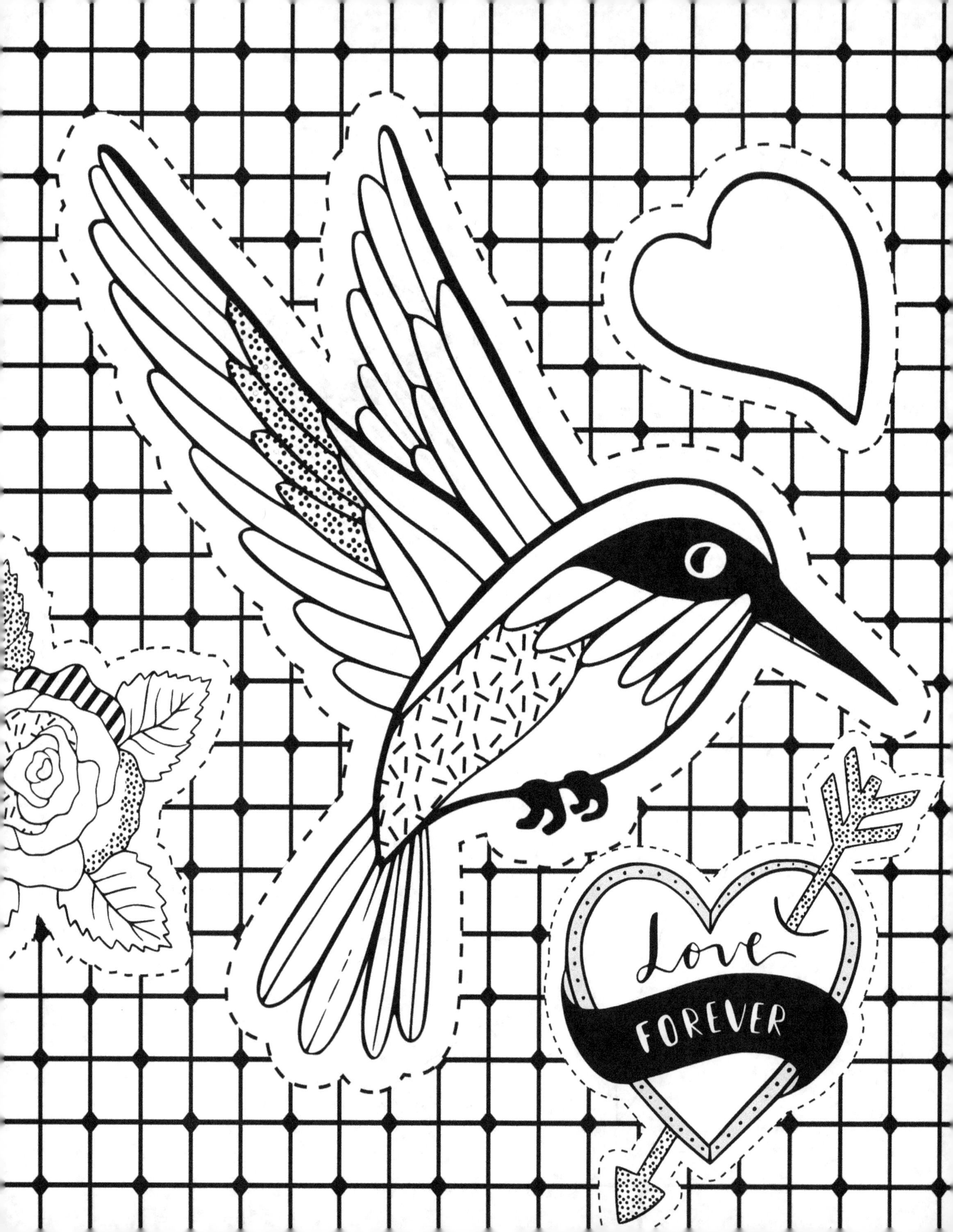
Love
FOREVER

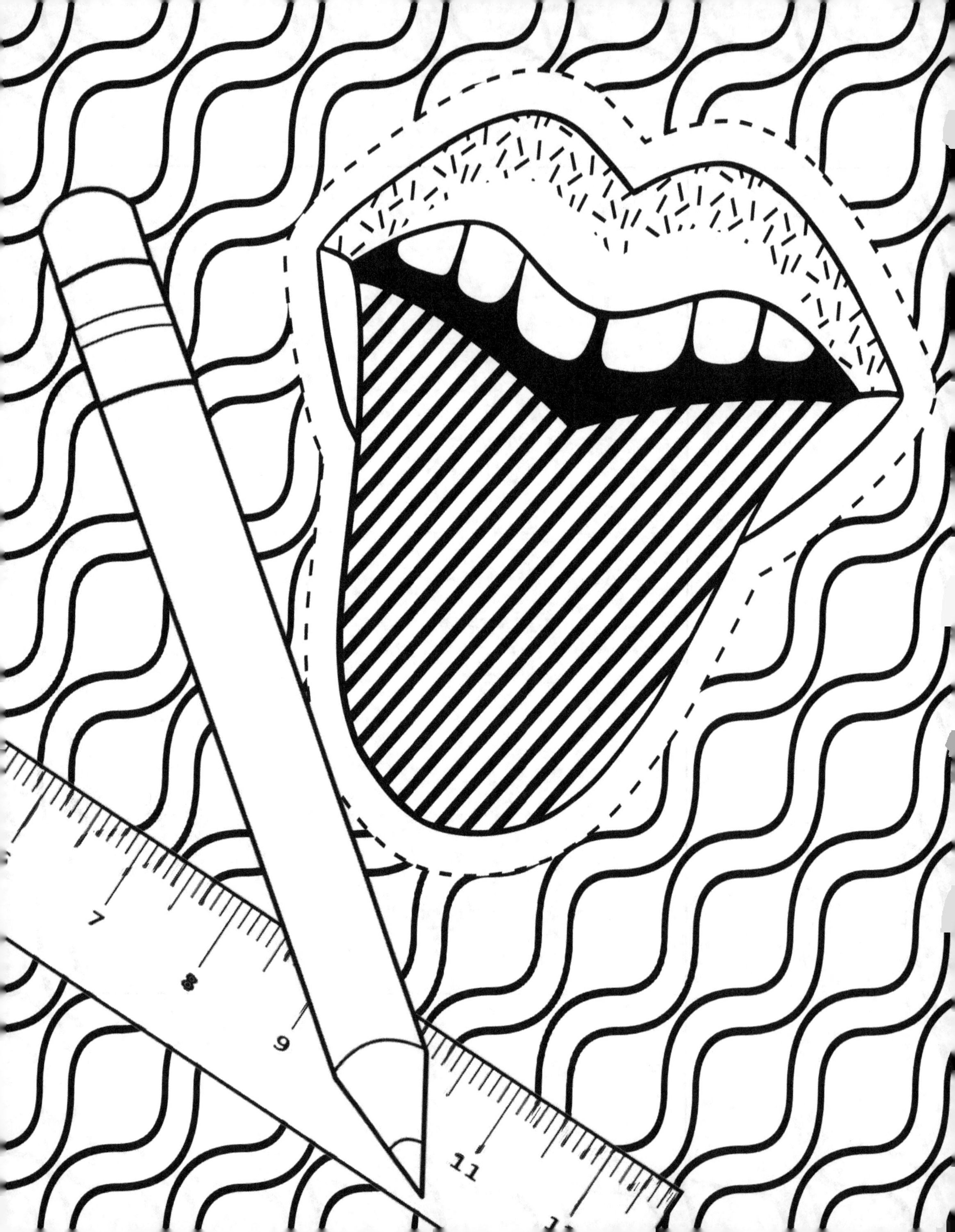
7
8
9
11

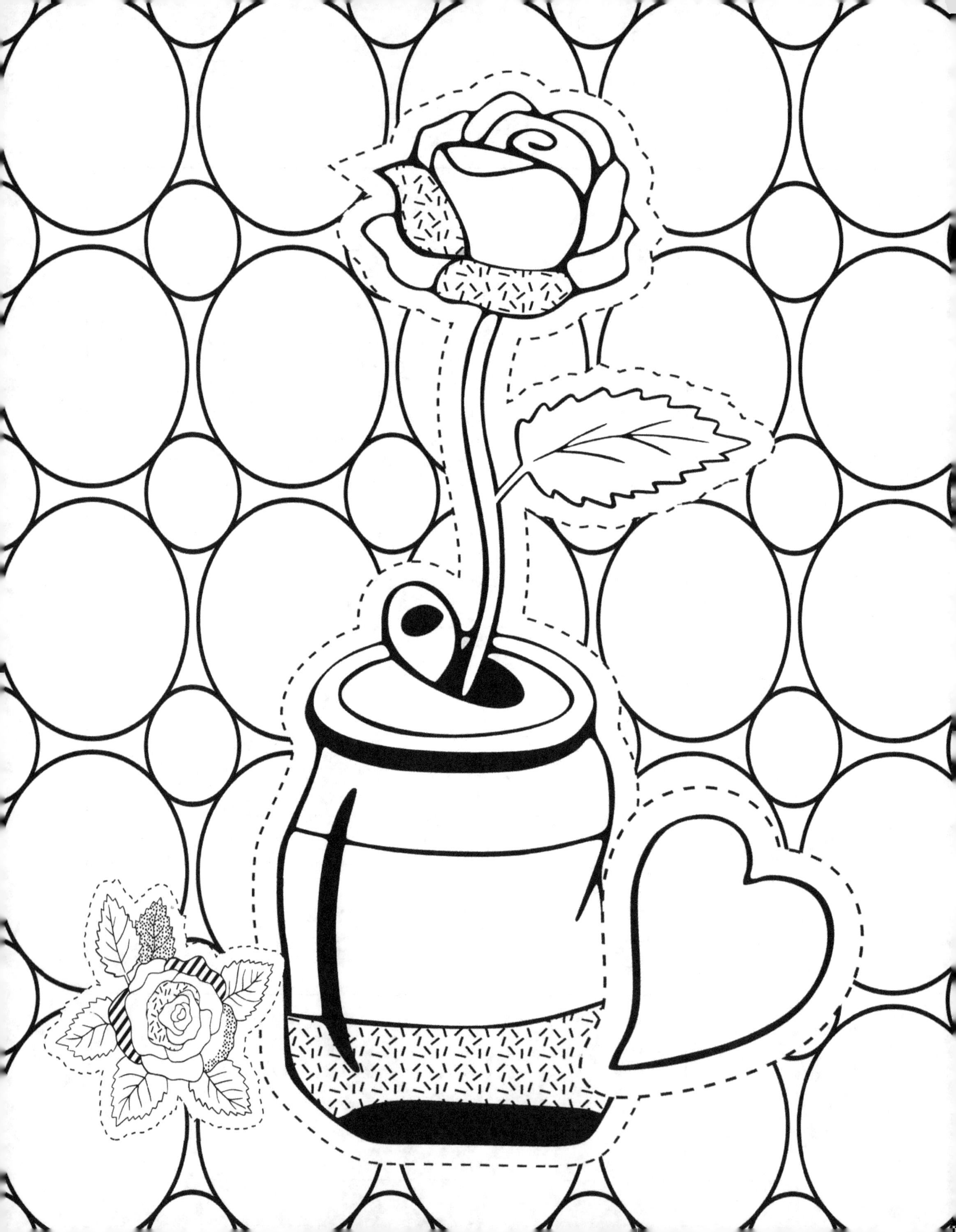

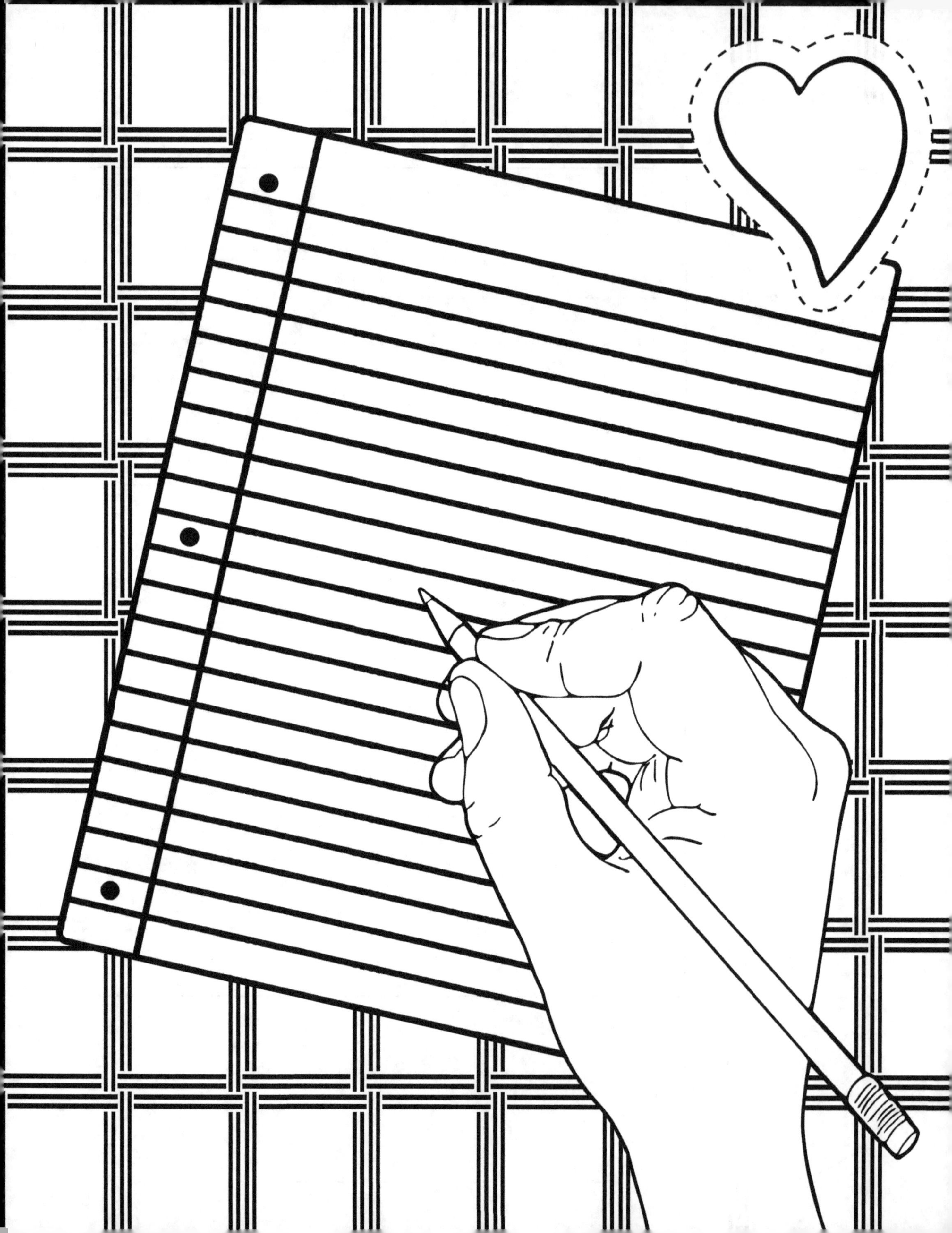

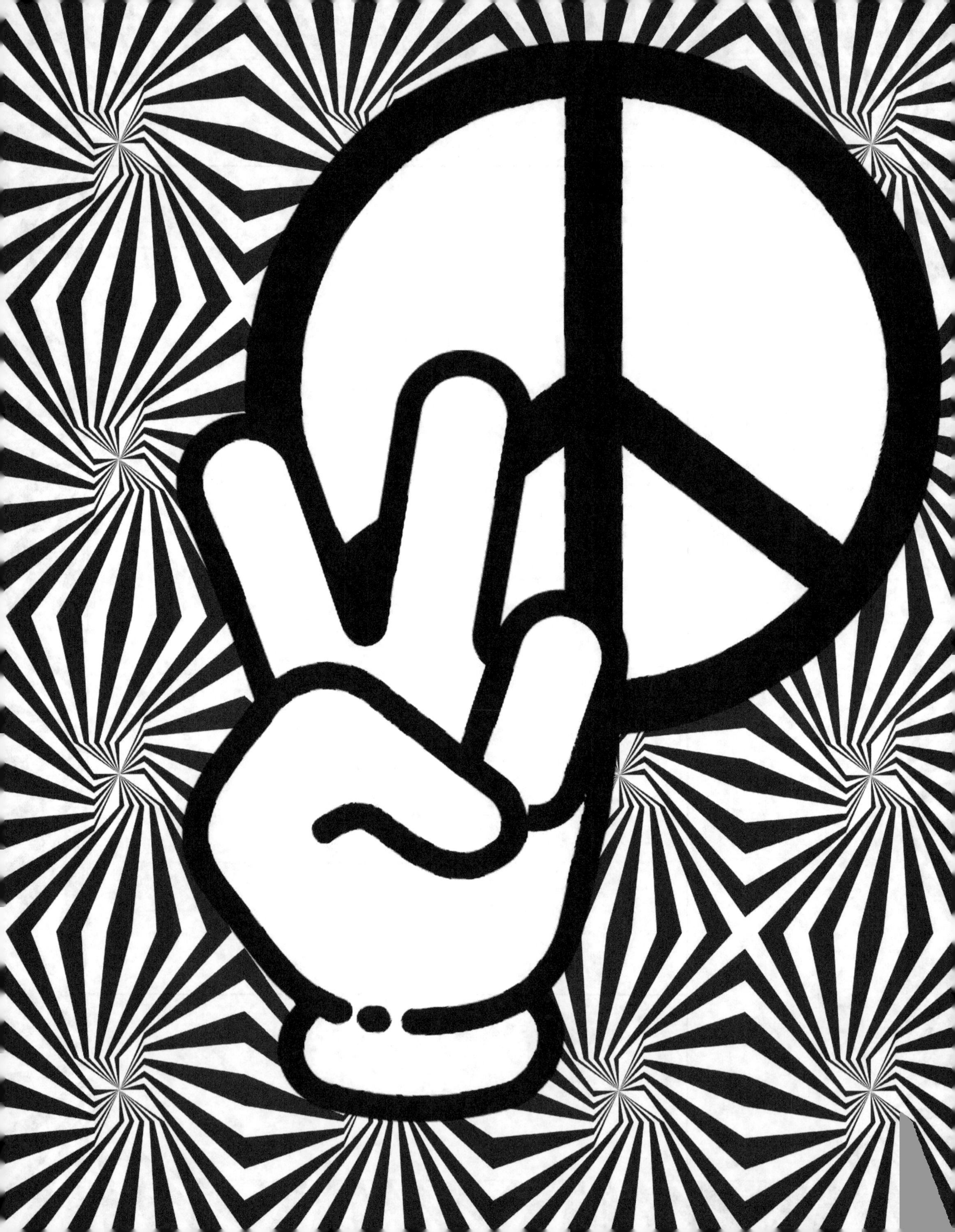

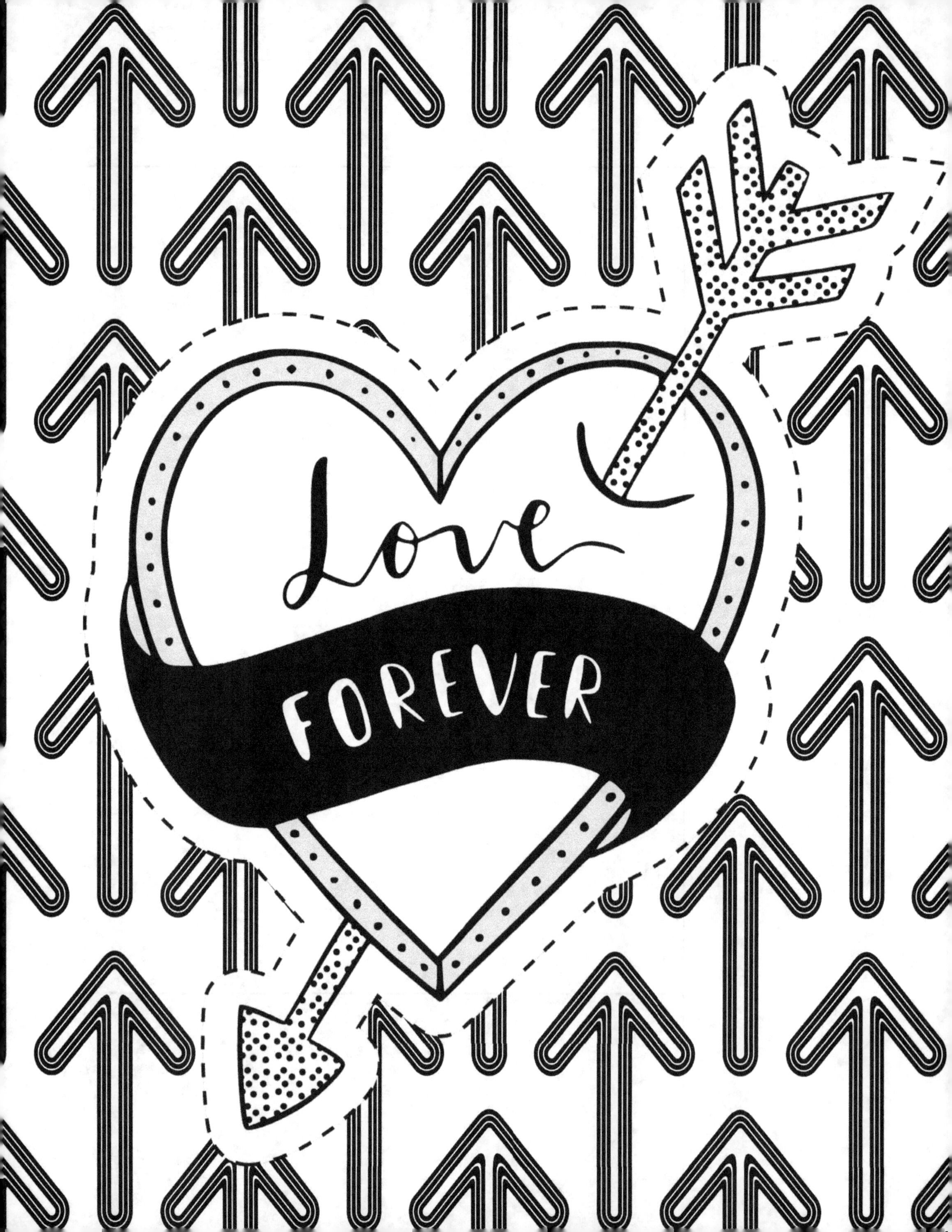
Love
FOREVER

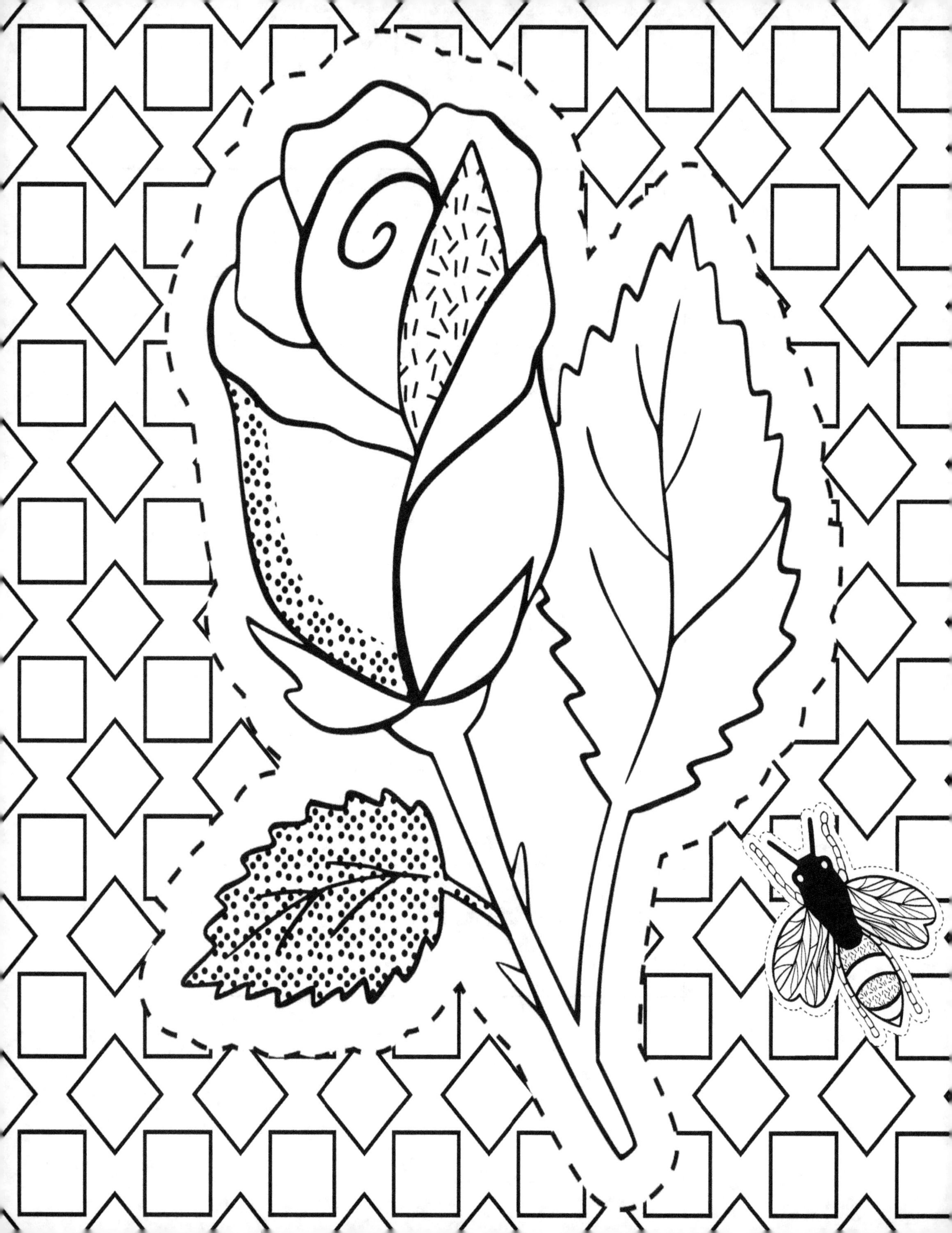

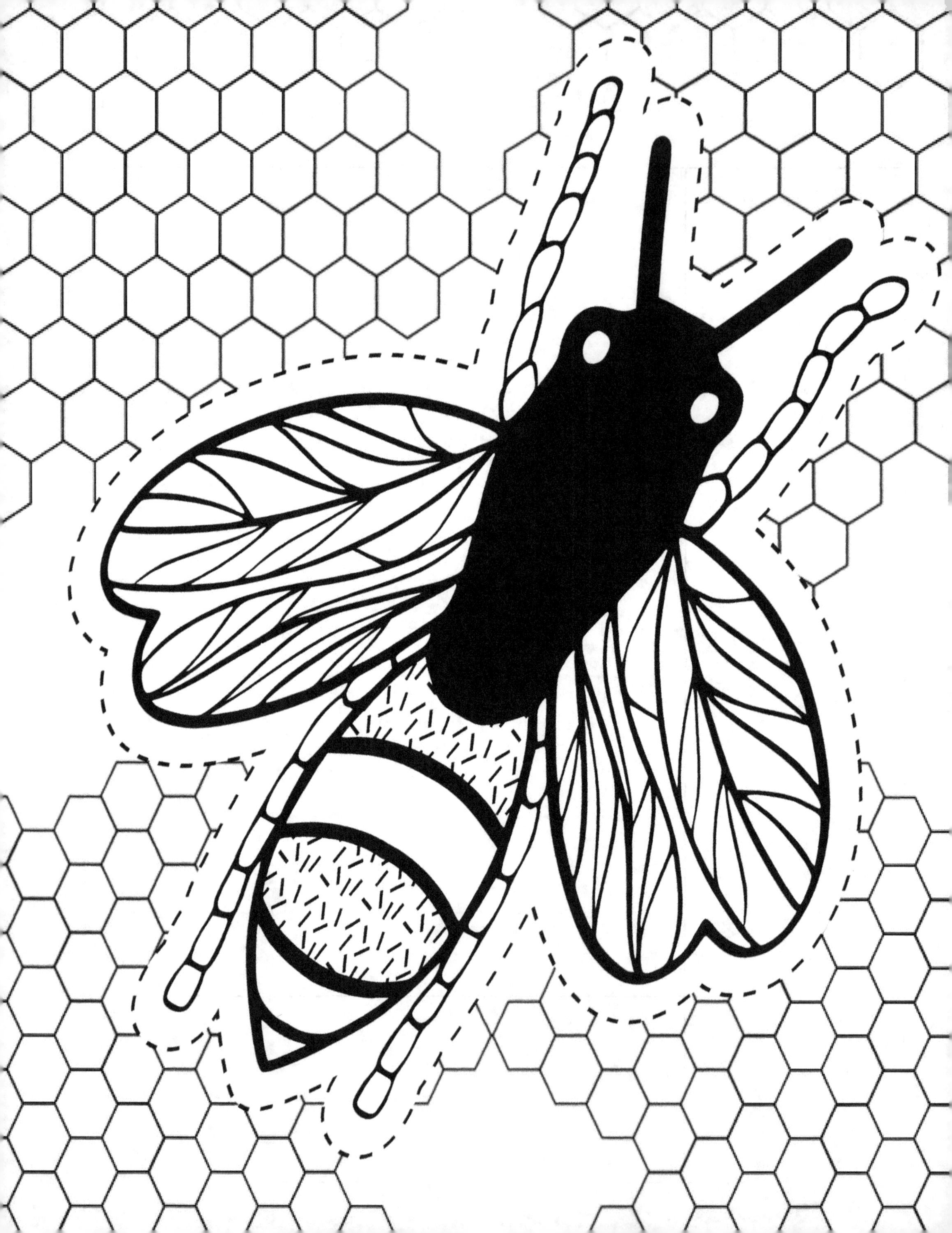

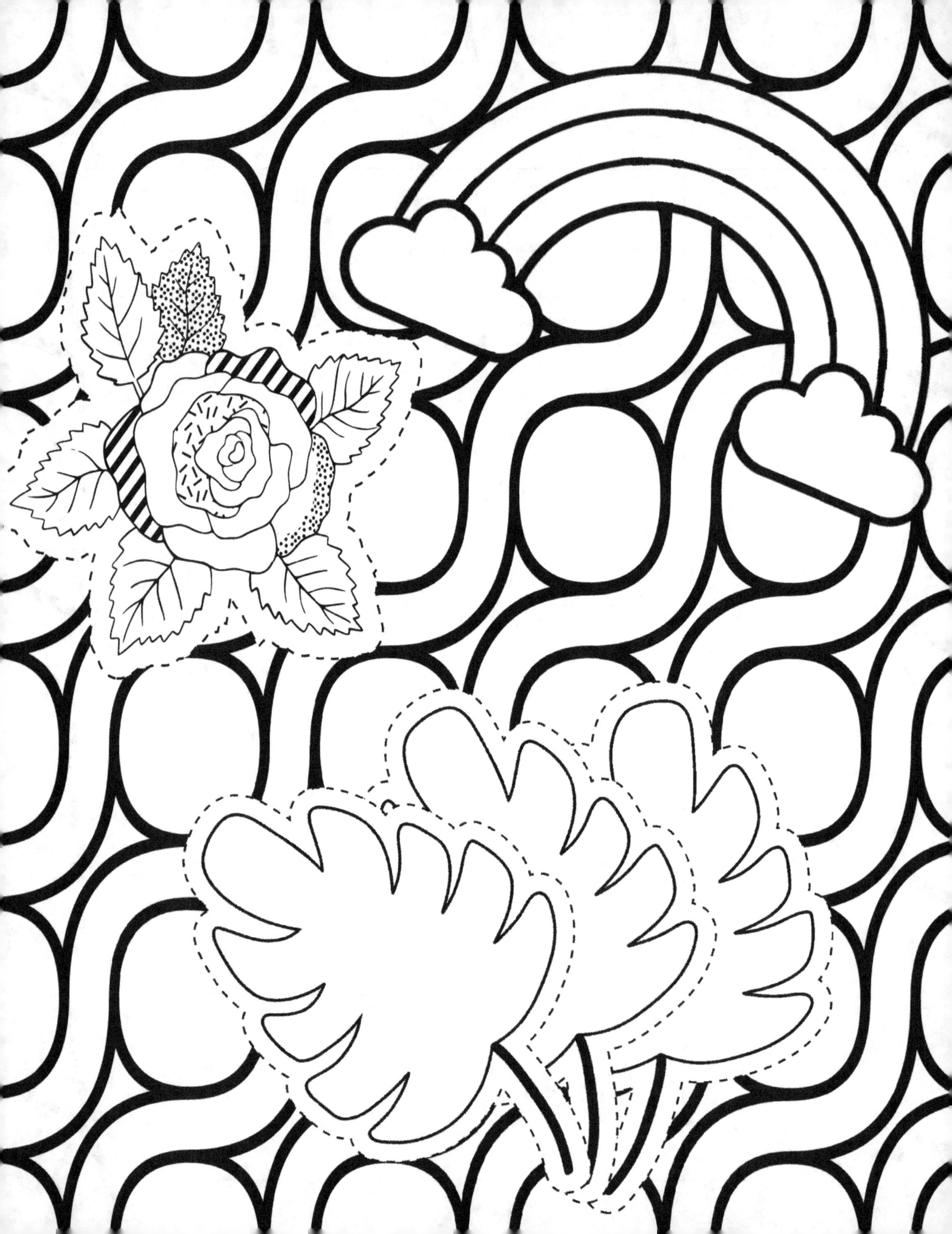

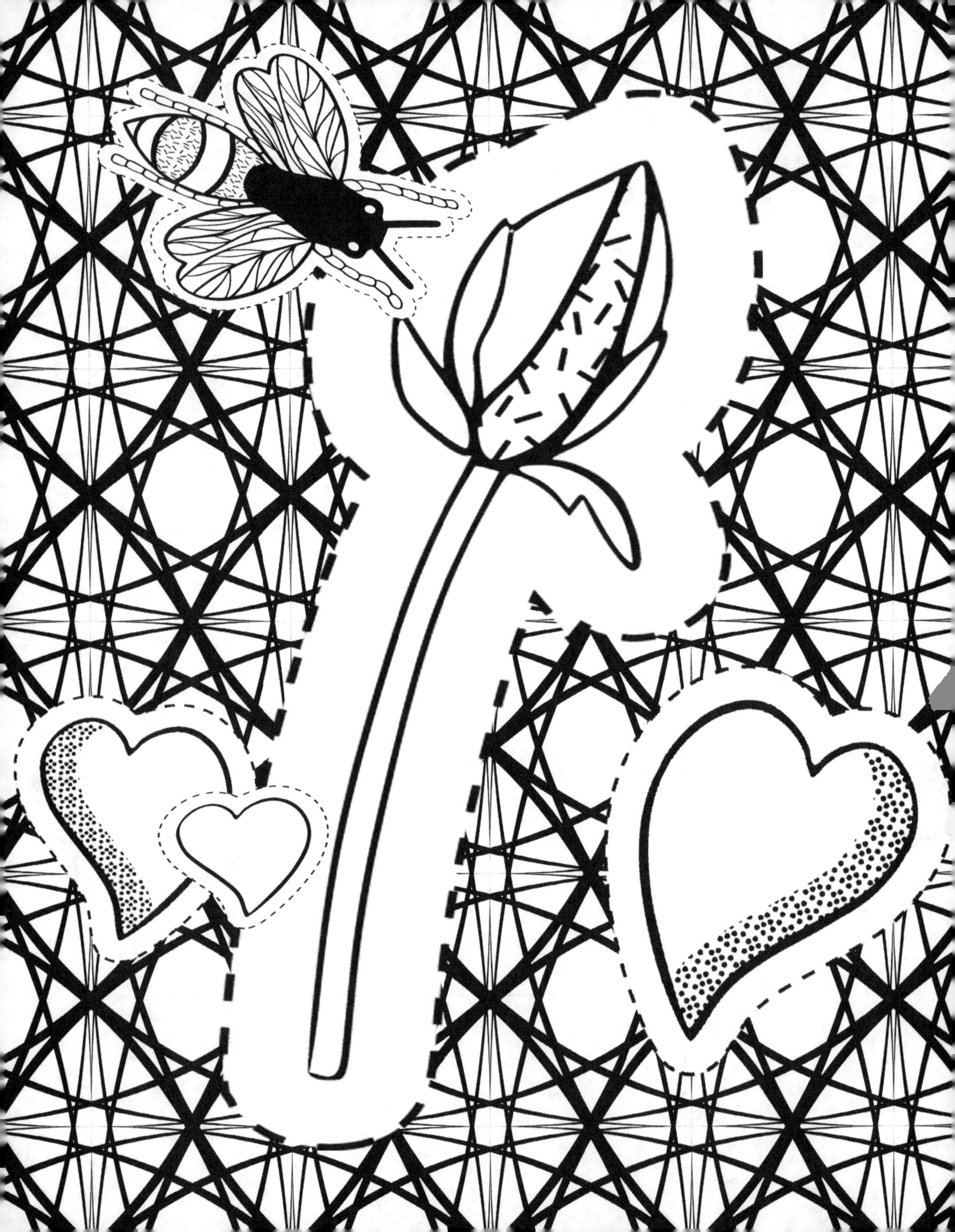

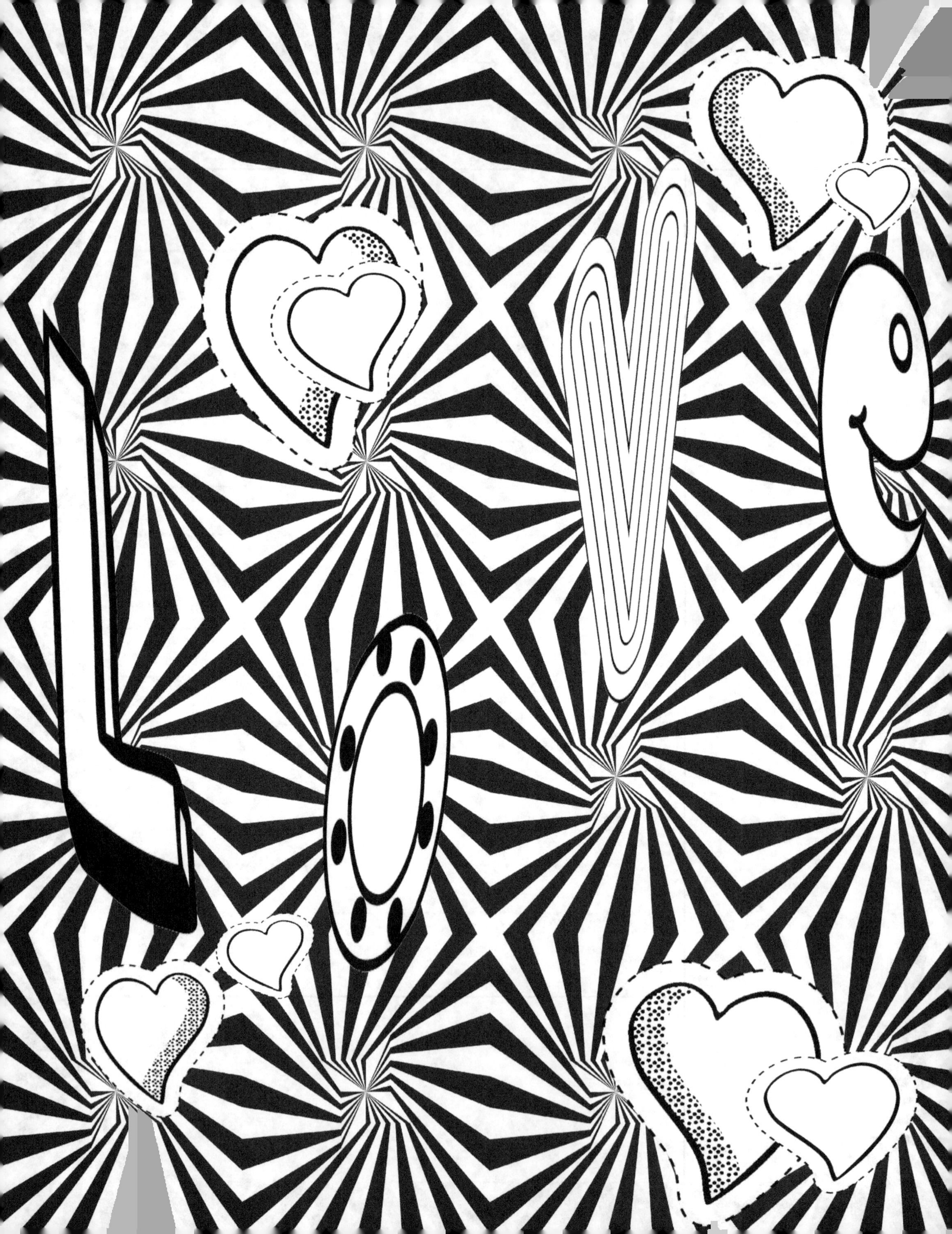
Love

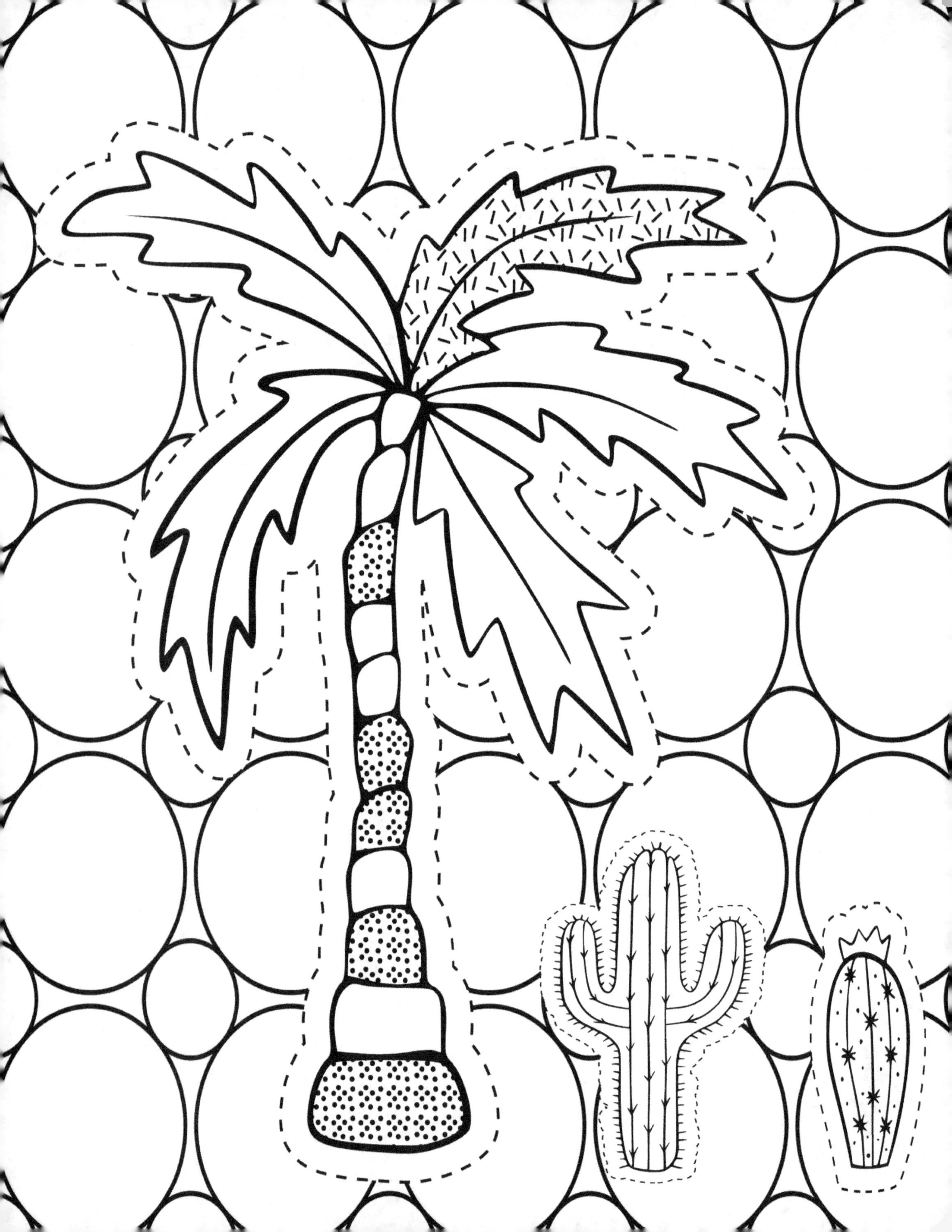

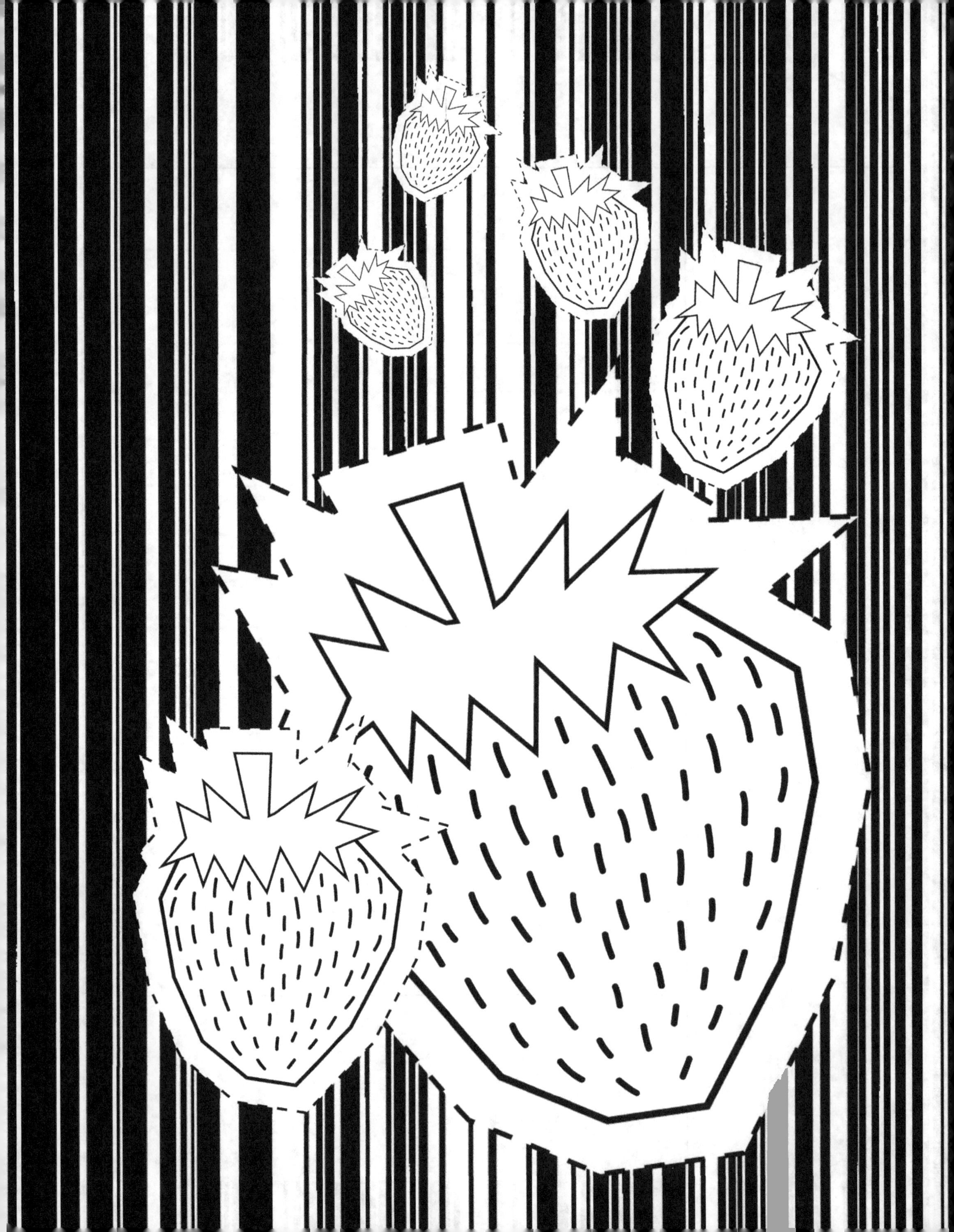

www.ingramcontent.com/pod-product-compliance
Lightning Source LLC
Chambersburg PA
CBHW080940170526
45158CB00008B/2325
9781081999841